Amazing Memories of Childhood

Mairi MacInnes was born in Co. Durham and educated in Yorkshire and at Oxford. Towards the end of World War Two she served with the WRNS. After marrying John McCormick, she lived in Berlin and then the United States. She has had awards from the National Endowment in the Arts and an Ingram-Merrill Fellowship. She received an Honorary Doctorate in recognition of her lifetime's work from the University of York in 2014.

Also by Mairi MacInnes:

Poetry
   Splinters: Twenty-Six Poems
   Herring, Oatmeal, Milk & Salt
   The House on the Ridge Road
   Elsewhere & Back: New & Selected Poems
   The Ghostwriter
   The Pebble: Old and New Poems
   The Girl I Left Behind Me: Poems of a Lifetime
   The Precipice
   Amazing Memories of Childhood and Other Poems

Fiction
   Admit One
   The Quondam Wives

Memoir
   Clearances

Amazing Memories of Childhood, *etc.*

Mairi MacInnes

First published in the UK in 2016 by Two Rivers Press
7 Denmark Road, Reading RG1 5PA.
www.tworiverspress.com

© Mairi MacInnes 2016

The right of the poet to be identified as the author of the work
has been asserted by her in accordance with the Copyright,
Designs and Patents Act of 1988.

All rights reserved. No part of this publication may be reproduced,
stored in or introduced into a retrieval system, or transmitted,
in any form, or by any means (electronic, mechanical, photocopying,
recording or otherwise) without the prior written permission of
the publisher.

ISBN 978-1-909747-15-9

1 2 3 4 5 6 7 8 9

Two Rivers Press is represented in the UK by Inpress Ltd
and distributed by Central Books.

Cover and text design by Nadja Guggi
Typeset in Janson and Parisine

Printed and bound in Great Britain by Imprint Digital, Exeter.

Acknowledgements
Some of the new poems collected here were first published in the
Hudson Review, *The Times Literary Supplement* and the *Yale Review*.
Others appeared in two pamphlets: *The Precipice* (Beeston: Eyelet
Books, 2010) and *Amazing Memories of Childhood and Other Poems*
(York: Stone Trough Books, 2014).

Contents

I

Hardly Anything Bears Watching | 3
The Present Tense of Machines | 4
I Look for You Everywhere | 6
I Object, Said the Object | 8
Reading Cavafy in Translation | 10
At Five the Train | 11
The Old Naval Airfield | 12
Plymouth | 13
Passion | 14
The Two-Man Saw | 15
Welcome to Mendocino | 16
A Linen Skirt | 21
Horses | 22
    1. The Racehorses at Saratoga
    2. Hambletonian, Rubbing Down
    3. The Cave-In
    4. The Fields of Light
November Digging | 28
Evening on the Estuary, Noon at Sea | 30
Luskentyre, Isle of Harris | 31
Travelling North | 32
Hard Lives | 34
A Landscape in the North Riding | 35
The Factory | 36
The Shock | 38
The Pebble | 39
In York Minster | 40
At Colonus | 41
Antigone at Colonus | 42
The Sparrowhawk | 44
Islay Goes To Sleep | 45
Otherness | 46
Voicing the Air We Breathe | 48
A Word of Acknowledgement | 49
The Sleeve | 50

II

Reasons | 53
Father Felipe | 54
Studley, 1940 | 55
Bread | 56
The Pet | 57
Bloomsbury Gardens | 58
Homeless | 59
Prey | 60
The Colour of Soldiers | 61
Waking | 62
Ataraxia | 64
Amazing Memories of Childhood | 65
    1. The Precipice
    2. Fog
    3. The Row
    4. The Storm
    5. Lowna
    6. The Hare
    7. After Her Funeral
    8. In Antwerp Once
    9. Those Evenings
    10. At Duncombe
    11. Fairbanks, Alaska
    12. Hindenburg

Hardly Anything Bears Watching

Hardly anything bears watching.
Bricks and stone
Have lost their intense surprise.
For years I kept my trust in things.

Even beyond the last parishes
Fringed with refuse,
Hills drown beneath the surveyor's rod.
They too lie perfectly numb.

The old parabolas of socialism,
Spirals of love,
Make hope the habitat of the soul.
But hope's not native to the blood.

No comfort from the boy who draws
Upon my memory of bombs.
The man recalls
Brave days on a far-off sea.

Picture after picture fails.
When I was young,
The pavement kerbs were made of stone,
A substance like my finger-nails.

It is not like that any more.
I do not see
The essential life of inorganic things.
Humanity has covered all.

The Present Tense of Machines

My friend Mercedes is neat by nature.
Neat rows of books she has, neat polished furniture;
Her floors are swept and bright.
Her mirror hangs exactly opposite
Pots of pink and green and white
Poinsettia, banked so the eye will settle
And flit, and yet return to mark a wrinkled petal
That if it fell might all disharmonise.

My friend Mercedes has also
Neat cushioned chairs, soft as the devil,
Drawn about a sofa table set with a silver tray.
And look, outside, almost outside the oval
Of the eye—neat picket fence, neat elm,
Neat roofs that cut a satisfactory line,
Neat sun to top the composition.

One day a cat came travelling through the grass,
And sensing he was watched, upreared his head.
Mercedes had her camera poised inside the house.
The pattern was dissolving in a dance
Of to and fro. Mercedes, if she was quick,
Might centre everything with one neat click.

At once the firehouse hooter gave a blast—
The cat ran off, the falling sun
Engulfed the clean-cut roofs in flame!
At least, Mercedes hoped, she'd caught the cat
Before his upraised head and glaring mask
Dropped and was gone. The rest was chaos, Mercedes said.

There is too much you cannot ask.
My friend Mercedes is neat by nature.
She absorbs the action any way she can.
There is always much left over.
Her photos please through strength of pattern.

Beyond their edges wildness rages.
But even within, there is a hint of hazard—
Movement already unpredictably moved in,
Where patterns form and gradually fail.

I Look for You Everywhere

Walking over the bridge early—
the level of the lake still sunk
in darkness, and the pale road
barely lifted out of the murk—
I found a man established
already at the parapet:
arms out, palms up, fingers fanned,
facing sunrise and a bank of trees
drab from the last week's heat.
He refused to turn at my footfall.
I trotted past him like a sheep,
resenting him. This was hardship,
to be sacrificed to his piety,
the penance in his ritual,
whatever it was. And instead of dawn,
solitude, and the lake scanned
for clarity as it reached the sky,
and land mysteriously seen re-born,
to have this lumber I'd no use for,
cramming a space meant to be bare!—
I still carry him, arms out, in my mind.

Last month, in Yorkshire, I hunted down
Charles Waterton's Walton Hall,
pillared and portico'd stone box,
brown paper colour, on its lake.
Brick houses now look down on it
from the Wakefield side. On the other hill,
a man ploughed up a great pale square
that grew dark as I watched.
And I recalled how Waterton
at the end of 1824
came back here from the Amazon
clad in top hat and old frock coat—
the pockets ideal for specimens
he was then to label and display
in glass cases, for visitors.

He made a sanctuary for birds
out of the Walton woods and lake.
I've read of him, in later years
he'd only to open his front door
and to extend his arms
and they converged from every cover
greedy to be fed: bevies at his feet,
wings on his chest, angel on hat,
two shoulders feathered thick,
and two armsworth of birds.
Nothing's left but house and birds—
widgeon, mallard, teal and coot,
pochard, Canada goose—manoeuvring
everywhere upon the moat.
His singular gesture folds to rest,
a butterfly shut in a book.

Now you're swimming in our pool.
Five laps of the same measure,
surging with steady uniform stroke,
and now you're limber, you emerge.
The water streams off your grizzled beard
and chest and thighs. You move with towel
to the luminous shade of the grape arbour,
a man getting on for seventy,
thinking of this and that, who chuffs
as he rubs the great coloured cloth
over the verdigris of his flesh.
Out in the sun the water heaves
in a glittering groping for what's gone.
Did it know what it had as I know it?—
that nakedness, that transfusion of life?
How easily now belief arrives,
and worshipfully claims nothing!

I Object, Said the Object

Out of the habit, I remembered nothing,
   Till, like a drunkard beating on the door,
     She shrieked out, 'More!' and more
        She had to have.
It was our anniversary. The devil longed
For rings and songs and coloured rocks and tinsel.

I wish the police would fix her.
   They'd end her screams with an axe's chop.
     What bliss to hear that yell lopped off!
        Think of the blank
Flowering, and then her coiffed acquaintance
Relishing her visceral history and sad finis.

I wonder now just how I could have picked her.
   Liable, was she reward? Her loss lobotomy?
     Was she the fundamental shifting at the eye
        Of penetrating pain?
Do magical mischances falter without her, the needle
In vision, for earth to pivot on, like an apple?

Whatever she meant once, appreciation's over.
   Today was bad. Tomorrow will be worse.
     Some hormone malady has made her haggish,
        Storming the stairs,
Mouth agog to the quivering uvula,
Taut hands like blown-up gloves waggling disaster—

Day after day I send for the doctor,
   And let his hollow needle intercept the kill.
     Thankfully I watch the boggling congeal,
        The blubbering less.
Sobered, she recovers rapidly,
Her eyes awash like two great silly puddles.

And then she swears she's never loved me more.
   She takes me in her big caress,
   Delicate diva, apt to bless,
      Hand on my head,
As if through blubbing we grow richer and closer,
Instead of always poorer and more cold.

But soon high-horsed again, she hops away,
   And sorry that I've let her be ridiculous
   And slow to monkey with the maladress
      That she displays,
I let her bolt and wander, and play herd
Upon the unsteady spending of her miscellaneous powers.

So it may happen, some night noble and serene,
   The last phut firework of her endeavour done,
   She'll turn, sane, cool, and say, 'Come,
      Bring down your sheep.
November's leaning on the fells, and Casseopia
Leans down to chant her song. Count your last lambs.'

Heartful and grateful then I'll bid them come,
   Their mouths like film stars' ravaged and remote,
   Uttering sounds unchosen, spontaneous, not
      Chidden, flocking,
My lambs, crowding to me, a stranger that says,
'What is it that you want? Is it this? Or this?'

Reading Cavafy in Translation

He would never have liked me,
A woman who's ample and hopeful and hardworking,
Bothered by sentiment, neither stylish nor austere.
Yet the loveless cadences of his translation
Warm me like an old friend from the capital
Met by chance on a provincial street.
His observations are witty and precise.
Like good stones in a jeweller's window
They give out fire.
They are the bounty of a fortunate life.
I understood too that the original contains
A familiar sadness about the civilisation
Falling away behind us, and a dry contempt
For our inept love of the present,
That flares sometimes, like beacons before Armada.
A clever fellow, he'd be amused to see me mourn
The sky's slow clouding over
And my loss of the good to come.

At Five The Train

At five the train left Hendaye
And trundled inland, across
The foothills of the Pyrenees,
Bound for Marseilles.

At dusk it drew up somewhere,
Earth dark, horizon high,
A greenness in the air,
And stars over the hills.

Half the passengers dismounted,
And doors slammed on crowds.
That's how we knew it was Lourdes,
That and the little fires
Carried up under the stars.

We sat in the dark carriage,
Broke bread and drank wine,
Until we couldn't see
What was flame and what star,
And the train took us off to Marseilles
In secret, as before.

The Old Naval Airfield

I looked out Henstridge lately,
somewhere where it always was,
even then, without maps or signs,
and thought of Philip, chief flying instructor,
brave Philip who soon was dead—
long ago, though, many years ago.

Pretty old, bosky old, footpath
country, and nothing was familiar
till suddenly the dull lane
roused me. A humpbacked bridge
over a disused railway led me
to B Camp that was: now a wood and a shed.
Opposite, the Wessex Grain Company—
storage silos that hummed
in the afternoon air like planes.
On the edge of the field, a bunker gradually
took my eye. A well-turfed barrow?
No, dear God, the rusted roof of a hangar
half-fallen in! And over the field, look,
Philip's control tower, a tall wreck
marooned in breaking waves of grass!

Survival is a form of murder.
My father ran round the garden in the dark
shouting, 'She's dead, and I could've
done more for her. I could have, and I didn't.'
She'd said earlier, 'He couldn't do more,
that man, best man who ever lived.'
Truth is, you can always do more.
You have to survive, that too, but it's murder.
He lived on, as you do if you can.

Plymouth

It could have been worse.
I'd missed my train on purpose
to meet my mother and say goodbye,
believing I mightn't be back for years.
Oh, folly, *folie de grandeur*! The next train ran late,
jammed with troops and dimly lit,
after eight hours entering Plymouth—midnight,
blacked out, bombed out, imaginary port
of embarcation for war. Shouts
of goodbye: the world emptied out;
a hiss and jolt and the slam
of doors and the reek of the spent engine.

So, a night by a gas fire tasting of metal
and the whispering tea-urn of the Salvation Army?
Rather pat with open palms the grid
of gritty brick walls that led
to the shut-fast Y and peal the dim bell.
Two women opened up and gave me hot milk
in the kitchen, while they watched, dependable,
hands in lap, and I drank like a calf from a pail.
My uniform skirt was covered in stains.
They looked and said nothing, for which I was grateful.
In the morning, the sun shone,
I went on my way to my Fleet Air Arm Station
believing I'd understood something,
which I hadn't. I arrived as I went on doing,
in an aftermath, when principle
turned awkward, and the air shook with refusal.

Passion

The passion of mourning I entered maturity with
was sullen, erotic, and atheist.
'So he hasn't written? Just as well.'
Without knowing him, my mother could tell.
She liked to play the malign goddess,
whipping up storms and thwarting Zeus,
but a third of the earth was burned,
a third of mankind murdered,
a third of the sea turned to blood—
what did she have to work on, or complain of,
but her glimpse of a single longed for thing
that might not want to be longed for, with my longing
vaster always than explanation.

When the truth came quietly into a crowded room
months later, it couldn't be hailed, or cried out for,
its features being already far too familiar—
and the demobbed man who gave me the news
only looked at me kindly, and was incurious.
I said at home: 'I heard he was killed.'
My mother barely paused. 'Perhaps it's just as well.'

'But only twenty-eight, and after five years of war,
accidently killed? That's not unfair
for a real hero, one of the best,
as everyone said? Don't you think it's a waste?'
That was the fact I thought might
convince her, but *fact* she would never admit.
So then I left her, unacknowledged,
and in private clung to my rags,
his birdwing smile, and enchanting air of belief
in me—too soon at odds with grief.

The Two-Man Saw

'You are cutting down a tree!'
Sagacious, in fresh cotton,
she advanced among the furious geese
to the edge of the lawn and the bald old elm
we were at work on.

'Do you know how to cut down a tree?'
We paused while she readied advice,
and over the clangour of geese
nodded as gay as we could, once more
a colonial couple in the wilderness,

and bent to the great Victorian saw,
one on each handle, rowing the huge
blade between us, one to the other,
as she watched, and the geese
extended their black nibs and hissed.

We were coated in sweat, you and I,
floured with sawdust, our eyes
starting and streaming with heat,
but how could we miss the sweet sap smell
that rose from the saw's stroke,

as of saint's blood, fragrant, incorruptible,
or not feel the elm's veer on its ropes
while, powered with regret, we sawed like maniacs,
and the saw bound, and came free,
and bound? And the instant before the elm

yielded and swayed down to the ground,
boughs a-crack, an unknown miraculous
virtue became manifest among us,
as if a hero had died
in an epic, in front of frightened squaddies.

Welcome to Mendocino

1

A tremendous sea, covered with experienced waves.
Crumbling sandstone cliffs, their rock lodes,
their lofty citadels, cut out and marooned.
Seaweed, sea lions, and a set of pelicans
assumed, and the sea passing them by,
a mastering element, the present controller.

But at Mendocino in the last century
the sea looked purely good.
It was what men had to sail on and fish,
and what brought ships there in the first place.
The land, too, looked good to mine and sow
and bear crops like other land. Accordingly
they built tall sporty houses in a spacious grid
right on the cove. The grand fronts
they painted pink, green, ochre, blue,
variously lit by the classical Pacific
flashing up the streets' divide.
A stroll through brambles to the shore
brought them a prospect of their neighbour
sea's abundance of colour and detail,
which made them smile, so well they understood.
They went home to add a superfluous fret
of wooden filigree to eaves and rails,
shingles cut and overlapped like scales on fish,
a delicate fan with glass over a door,
an outside staircase twined like morning glory.

2

The wayfarer runs his Honda up One
some ninety miles, half a day from San Francisco,
just to sleep in an old brass bed and eat breakfast
at one of the new inns of famous Mendocino.
The embroidered sheet turned down so bravely O,
the comforter and three lace pillows, their puffed feathers.

The bathtub with brass taps and lion paws.
The frilly white curtain. Old elephant cypresses
outside, flouncing their own black lace.

And soft as the light, womanly warmth up the mahogany stair.
Coffee, and biscuits baking. A pink appliquéd table cloth,
pots of honey and jam, fluted cups, zinnias in a jug.

Silver spoons. Knives with bone handles.
China plates wreathed with painted ivy.
The November sun of an old lamp.

*

Pin thin, the innkeeper in her tight blue jeans
and her sky-blue T-shirt and running shoes.
Her body bends in an arc like a tossed net

as she stoops to the sweet-breathing old black oven
and takes out six bread tins
filled with her own version of zucchini bread.

*

Down through the grid the tourist, touched with fire.
Sunlight shoots from the experienced sea.
His eyes prickle. His wallet's heavy.
He'd live here too if he had the money.
He'd thrum with artisans in an atelier,
ankle-deep in shavings, and make fine things.
He muses from shop to shop and buys expensively,
the sea at his back, the malign neglected sea.

*

Outside each shop, baskets of geraniums
bright in their crowd of leaves.
A hard wind from the sea. The flowers freshen.
Pretty red petals lick the sidewalk bricks.
But near the dump and its fallen fence
amaryllis as in Greek Sicily,
fleshy amaryllis all in pink,
pink trumpets with a golden tongue

in fullest voice, amaryllis on the fields of Etna,
belles of the ancient world. 'Naked Ladies,'
frowns the prim innkeeper, and slashes off their heads.

    3

Unionised labour's gone inland,
gone to the back country,
where the sea is musing and gentle,
far up a river where the tide turns
among trees and fields and mills;
the only knowledge of the sea now
is a slightly moving, tearing bite,
the single symptom of flamboyance.
It's quiet element for loggers
who float huge trunks in booms
and tether booms to stakes in watery roads
in a basin broad as a town;
who live by the close light of a wood
in houses the colour of old fish,
discarded catch chucked out on a shore.

    4

Here come the two Marys in their Toyota.
They've pawed through the merchandise. They're angry.
The stuff's meant for someone with more money.

The shopkeepers, though, wore a nuptial look.
'Goodness, how I loved my mother,' their young men's
little smile said, as if they handed over

a priceless trinket no Mary wanted in her young days
but should be glad of now. But Mary has Mary,
half blind though the one is and the other wheezes.

So what's the sea been up to?—clambering
through briars and paper wrappers down to the cove
where the sea's whimpering, spilling and moping.

Its quake-strewn ramparts of huge stones
meet expectations as always and as the Marys do,
since it is without necessity,

the sea, two-thirds of the earth's surface
but not marketable; unconserved; not taken into account;
even its fine storms improperly assessed, often,

and, unpredicted, called natural calamities,
as if that nailed them. The sea, admired,
becomes admirable, and gratis to the point of tears,

like the moose that wandered past the back door once,
in Maine, two calves at heel as big as trucks,
the three of them sauntering into a Mary's life

as if they were safe there for good.
What if the beach tilts against the eyeball,
coming down, black visor over white metal,

and the other's breath is slapped hard with grit
till she gasps? The magnificent unplaced desire
at liberty here has them amused.

The sea becomes their spokesman, mouthing its vowels
between their toes and shoulder-high out there,
it pushes its roars and chirrups into their ears,

it slides wet and heavy into their hands.
And its floor—not like a kitchen floor's
aberration in dirt and stains, but single,

whole, total. Its stones, now,
sweet to hold, round and heavy,
that the sea has rolled in the river mouth,

even dried, they smell faintly of the sea.
The Marys forage for some that are perfectly round.
They're at home here, with their old measure,
the skin come off the rest of the world.

5

Chaperones with huge beach towels
held out for naked bathers,
in the cool of the garden where the stones will go,
the lords of language with their nets and
globed silences, placed exactly,
with many a considerate cocking of the head
and standing back to observe the effects.
Bougainvillea, jasmine, ivy, myrtle,
and other jabberers with coloured hats
advance with their paraphernalia of roots
as the garden sways at its anchor—
the perfectly round stones of Mendocino
brought back by the two Marys.

6

The sea grumbles far away, the sea devoid of honour
as it is, gobbling, dangerous, cold, for ever
missing something, it doesn't know what.
'Oh, for God's sake,' it cries, and bellows all night
through the lace curtains of the famous Mendocino inn.
What if the only thing wrong is the moon?
The sea wants its words too, to declare that
it is various and detailed and craves to be looked at,
and gives of itself for ever. It only imagines it is hungry,
full as it must be with continent wolfed.

A Linen Skirt

The flax grew in the field
   So the skirt was tough.
From the first it had the weave
   And hand of field-grown stuff.

But I bit into a peach
   And juice ran down my chin.
I promptly washed the skirt
   But the mark stayed in.

The skirt bleached pale as cream
   And dried a shade of toast
Except where the juice had fallen
   Where pinkness had set fast.

I cut my finger next
   And drops of blood fell down.
The skirt bleached white as lint
   But the blood turned brown.

Red as a crayfish, then,
   And russet as a bird,
Whatever dyes I chose
   The peach and blood stains showed.

Yet I wear it with delight
   And smile when the colours fade,
Because the weight and weave
   Show something flax has made.

Marked as the palm of my hand
   Where experience is revealed,
Because, I like to think,
   The flax grew in the field.

Horses

1. The Racehorses at Saratoga

Six thirty in August, sun over the smudge of night,
ten horses on the practice track,
blobs that trace the curve against the woods—
and here they come towards us into the straight,
floating like cavalry out of the haze,
fanned out, controlled, in twos and threes,
hoofs snapping earth, fore and then hind,
bodies aslant to fit the overlap,
heads coiled high on necks, pulled up,
made to contain their cresting energy.
On one, a woman stands upright over the saddle,
braced by twelve-inch stirrups, cut-out angel
with bud breasts and a bug helmet
facing the warm and stifling wind.
Her legs bridge the ebb and flow of the stride
more like charioteer than rider,
till just where we stand at the rail, she
folds like a landing frog and reins,
then thrusts—the horse bursts from the start,
head flung out, legs paired off along the diagonal.
Release, release! Involuntary shout
from two spectators hanging on the rail!

And now, the horse returns with his tough rider
with the leathery face. She dismounts,
swaggers as she leads him in, and as
his sloping gait falters and he checks his stride,
she shouts and belts him with the reins.
He jerks his head and makes the curb chain clink.
Now she unsaddles him and walks him round the ring.
He's rubbed, shampooed and sluiced and blanketed.
And then the leathery women and stunted men
drift off to breakfast under a tin roof.

By noon, men have raked and sprinkled the track,
painted the pavilions white and gold
and coped the copper roofs and planted geraniums
beside the pebble paths. The next day swarms
with Vanderbilts, Mellons, Whitneys,
punters and touts. Jockeys in flaming silks
mount horses bred three centuries for this.
The grandstands flutter their ten thousand flags.

What is this residue you feel, of burnt-out shame?

2. Hambletonian, Rubbing Down

George Stubbs's tender portrait
of the great racehorse Hambletonian
shows him after his four-mile race
with Diamond, which he won
for an enormous wager, some say
at the price of never racing again,
he was so broken. The canvas is huge,
and brown Hambletonian fills it
from top to bottom, side to side.
We look through his legs
to Newmarket Heath and a shed.
In the foreground, though, his eye
is bloated, his flanks froth, his mouth
jerks on the bit as he turns and looks
straight at the painter, George Stubbs,
now in his seventy-sixth year.

The horse half-raises a hoof to strike
the stable-lad crouching under his neck
as he gingerly rubs him down.
A dwarfish trainer holds the reins—
a top hat nests on his ears,
a frock coat falls to his heels.
As against the comic appearance
of his clothes, however, his face
is bright and serious, as if he and Mr Stubbs
share some intelligence.

Eighteen hundred. Pitt is Prime Minister,
Napoleon First Consul.
The wars with France, led by Napoleon—
First Consul or Emperor—
will drag on umpteen years,
but old George Stubbs in his studio
is painting a broken horse.

3. The Cave-In

What did he say, that blinded dusty boy
when he was dug out?—
                      that first the darkness
of the cave-in lay identical, outside and in,
across his eyelids; that the cries
he shrilled met stone and cried back to him
as echoes. He was imprisoned by an entire hill.
So humble and colossal it was, he cried until
the cold stationed in his boots wormed up
to his armpits, and threaded itself on vertebrae
and folded round his belly as a web.
So his tears dried up in convulsive shivers;
the taste of salt and tannin dried out his head.

When he came to, he heard thumps—
his heart perhaps, or a pavement tamper,
and increasingly nearer, a flutter of water,
a streaming, pounding, a clatter of hoofs
that halted almost on top of him. He knew the advance
of a heavy animal, he smelled sweet grass
on its breath, and acrid hairiness of hide,
before he felt on his ears the bloom
of huge warm lips, tenderly, curiously applied,
and the nudge of damp nostrils on his neck,
and recognised the pushiness of a great beast
used to its own success.
                      He got up (he said)
oh, joyfully, and touched the warm and rounded moleskin
that shut in tons of brilliant flesh,
and felt it glide under his hands, and twitch, ticklish,
till in a gigantic snatch it bolted off
slap into the rock, and there the skull and skeleton
sparked like a lode, or a luminous fossil,
the bones of a horse running; while he heard,
a good way off, the noise of hoofs.
What a horse was doing there, what it meant,
he'd no time to wonder before the rescuers
broke through the rockfall and found him.

4. The Fields of Light

Again and again, a presence in the clearing
that was the clearing itself,
the row of firs in snowy quilts.
the parting of sky and snow.
Again and again, the cold unpainted room,
the dead fire, the tap's needle of cold,
the cooling skins of the bed, the kettle's fuss,
the bang and commotion of the furnace.
Twigs kindled, waggling fingers of warmth.
The days began by writing themselves.
Dark words ploughed the fields of light.

In the afternoon, in the riding barn,
old William waited: twenty-eight years old,
plump in his baize winter coat
ancient and patient and horse. Round and round
the riding barn among the competent
petulant well-mounted little girls
thumped William, reliable Pegasus
for the reliable winter poet.
Later, blown, the unsaddled William
examined his stall, munched hay, propped a hoof.
He may have remembered Homeric gallops,
leaps, falls, great treks home in rain
after getting lost, long miles from home;
or that was the poet, steering a metal vehicle
 back to the rented cabin in the woods.

On the very last day, the firs written up,
the snow, the fires, the light and dark,
and William, all caught and bound,
the poet drove out of the clearing in the trees
to where the route for the city
zippered up the divided woods,
the fields of snow, the icy marshes,
the great lovely vistas opened down valleys.

But a mile or two out, there was William
entering the highway from a country lane
at full gallop, riderless, tail high as a flag,
two silly colts along, a band of marauders
drunk with merriment, that sent the traffic
braking, parking, flashing hazard lights
while elementary horseplay went on—
such bucking and cavorting, squeals and nips!
A poet could scarcely believe it.

Then, rapture spent, William permitted a running girl
to catch up, and submitted to a halter
and so walked home to the barn, the colts
trotting obediently at heel—but not before
he had let out a neigh like a clarion
and produced a prodigious buck, to show
the drivers edging into the flow of traffic
how unreliable he was, how original,
how easily he broke the dark lines
the poet had laid over the fields of light.

November Digging

I am cutting the clearing free from its roots
>   *Garden* will float
free from the adventitious
>   the glistening goutweed suckers
ganglias that sprout nettles
>   ivy's furred hawsers
the fibrillations of bramble

Sweet light tents me as I fork
>   yet what mote flits
into the corner of my eye and out
>   hides and reappears and hides
a small brown knowing bird
>   drawn to an exposé of flies
three sharp notes
>   but there again he hides

When the black crumb's clear
>   I'll plant bushes
gooseberry blackcurrant raspberry
>   and one day cheat him of their fruit
punnets of soft
>   emerald onyx ruby
for all the pies of summer

But in the interim I fork up
>   knobs of clenched bulbs
snowdrop garlic aconite
>   and china in blue and white
chipped lustreware and famille rose
>   crude pottery with painted bands
a flint sharp as a knife
>   a horseshoe oxshoe hinge key bottle
five four-inch nails handmade
the upper of a boot
>   who lives down there to need such things

Would he hear if I sang out
        and push up through the soil
his two white hands to clasp my neck
        and show his white face for a kiss
a kiss that would taste of raspberries

Evening on the Estuary, Noon at Sea

For Esteban Vicente, painter, on his eightieth birthday

The estuary is violet
among its reeds and bars.
The field of the evening holds
in the crown of the sky.
It's dark on the bare hills.
Ash drifts thick in mile-wide smears
far out at sea—drift emptying content
where the long waves disappear:

And I remember riding out of Orkney
on the ferry to Scrabster—
three tides meeting and a buckling ship;
tumult and froth below;
aloft, gull-escorted mast and the brave flags.
It was midsummer in the far north,
the air very bright,
the wind hard at work—
so much haled out of the fabric of matter
and tuned like matter, luminous,
excited by present arrival in Caithness.

Here, as darkness fills out,
absolute circumstance also
begins to bloom.
The colours of land and water
grow deep in reflected light.
Here and in your painting, Master,
what's allowed will happen.
The eye arrives alone at its centre,
its eventual passion.

Luskentyre, Isle of Harris

Big easy Luskentyre lies at the great sea.
Its bones are stone ledges,
its pelt the stir of bent grass;
its fingers reach for an island,
a last one, drawn tight and tall
against a sea whetted
by knowledge of full-bodied Luskentyre.
There gulls work the rock.
From there as the wind turns inland
late on a summer evening,
they heel in the slipstream silently
as night fills the space on the ground.

I balance here too, thinking of nothing,
not of the tide I saw,
nor Luskentyre's retreat under the night:
it is all so much wished for—
the owl hooting over the water,
near me a heron on its one leg.
The owl cried as I drove the narrow road.
I got out at the beach
and walked barefoot on the cold sand.
The sea purred. The headlands were lidded
in light. They waited and watched.
No impediment at last, no dross,
but in its own good time
the ear filling with the sea
and that owl on its dark continent
across from big easy Luskentyre.

Travelling North

The hills step forward.
I am nearly home
at residue: desperate, derelict;
what lies on its back
in the thick of the wood
between two billows of field;
what hides and sulks, the dud, the fool,
indifferent to rescue.

Now it's running for dear life
with its chimneys alive and dead
and mess of roses and clematis
crawling all over the roof.
What a sight! It is pitiful!
If I catch it I'll give it what for,
and I bet it is filthy,
I bet it can hardly see out,
I bet I'll arrive too late
and it'll just be quiet, big-eyed, shrunk.

Here is order, here in passage.
I take a fix on outlying farms'
single brightnesses.
A thousand sheep glimmer along the bank,
all meant, all bargained for.
I storm up in third gear
and look back on a plain
so vast it must contain everything.

Woods, fields, smoke, haze stretch
its pattern to the cathedral towers
and the two power stations'
five cooling towers each,
twenty miles away,
arguments from the silence
under my hissing tyres
repeated again and again as though
I do not take them in.

Another ridge, and I plummet down
between high field edges
in ever tighter curves, to a bend
where the odour of muck
sticks, like a sleeping pig,
and there my windows shine
out of their stone and oak
beyond the beech tree and the garden,
beyond the garth, beyond the farmer's
last retaining hedge, beyond this business.

It's deathly still in the yard.
Someone is shrinking into the dark
like a fool biting its thumb,
and someone already there,
daemon or boss or child,
grown tall and critical
is waiting to put me straight.
The fire will indeed be trim.
Can't I hear the furnace roar?
The beds will be white as brides,
new bread will be hardening,
the sloes disperse in gin
their bluish pungent smoke,
July's hard pickled plums
soften to apricot.

Yes, then, I've been wrong,
oh far too frequently,
made stupid mistakes, got drunk,
become unmanageable, gone off
without compunction.
What is the difference?—I'm back.

The house is waiting, a golden woman.
Her arms are folded, she wears
her contemptuous filial grin.
I'll get out the luggage, go in.
Dear house, I love you best.
Receive me ever kindly as you do now.

Hard Lives

It was foggy and frosty, not a night to be out,
and there was no one in the village street,
and nothing moved ahead on the lane
that led between Stocking Farm and larch plantation.
Grass on the verges stared like the fur of some arctic animal;
the fog came up like a wall at eye-level
and sagged around us like curtains.
We drove right through it. After all it was easy,
this getting home in winter, we could give lessons

up to the second when roe deer shot over the headlight tunnel
in the arc of the wipers: left to right funnelled
leaping grey creatures with delicate wet black
eyes and muzzles—and we cried out in shock,
that thinned into pleasure because they were free of
the world, and their lives were apart, and their exit as soft
as bolt after bolt of silk tossed to the floor
of the wood and unravelled. The way ahead was wretchedly bare,
pot-holed macadam going uphill between fences.

We'd stopped with a jolt. As we re-started, as
I shifted the gears one by one, as we lost
the fog, climbing, we saw the measure of frost
stretched over the open field,
the empty barren January field
(but we'd be home before we questioned anything).
Red eyes in the headlights, shiftings, pale flickerings:
those were just sheep, solid wool bodies, imbecile faces,
mouths crammed with hay (plenty more hay strewn on the grass).

It was only days later it hit me how false
perception had been and how misery, what else?
drew the roe deer from the wood: so famished
they fed with the farmer's sheep, so vulnerable they fled
at the crunch of the car; and more, the world we despised
was open for them to take refuge in
as it wasn't for us, who weren't secretive, or starving.

A Landscape in the North Riding

First there's the map: earthwork and tumulus
lettered in gothic by the mapmaker;
rivers, farms, woods, hills, lettered in roman
and named by those who by now are nameless.

The rest is partial, like childhood.
It's a splinter from the first self
needling under the skin, as something needles
under these placid pasturing hills.
It's a kestrel soaring up lanes
so the seam opens between fields,
and hell's beyond, a chasm of mud and water.
It's the end of a lane in the wood,
at a clearing empty as a pot,
a sky on it like a blue enamel lid,
on the other side a disused blackthorn tunnel
with rail ruts a foot deep from traffic
that passed there before macadam,
and pencillings through winter pasture,
beyond, where the way rounds a contour—
not the ruled line of the car road,
stiff as a copy, but a curve yielding the weight
of hoofs and feet and endless thought.

The path photographs that thought:
let it be sombre, excessive, revolutionary;
reversal in mind, not rescue.
Recall that a hero went off, promising to write,
and instead came hiatus. Was it death,
that long silence while it rained and was dark?
He returned long ago. It was spring.
These fields knew the truth all along,
where he strayed, among these insurgencies,
these woods with their signs and guns.

The Factory

Big turgid beasts, we climb stone steps

to the cavernous fourth floor of the old factory
where heavy machines once stood in rows
worked by hundreds of women, long-skirted women,
women with soft hair looped high on their heads,
who would have pursed lips and swopped glances
at the very sight of us, audience as we are,
leisured, idle, and censuring:
though now on this empty waxy skyblue floor
there's a sudden start of light on the emptiness,
falls of air from wall-high windows, mirrored
against walls opposite, shot from the icy skies
of wintry Manhattan, through screens of glass
set on curtain walls' metal and stone.
Cast-iron pillars indoors hold floor and ceiling apart
in nineteenth-century factory style, made over
for us of the twenty-first century,
each pillar bandaged against hurt flesh,
wrapped and padded against dancers' fall,
and here along the edge we sit, old
toads, the lot of us, along the mirror,
conscious of our soft bellies,
tender squashy feet, and jewelled eyes,
and wait: all we're good for.
Now the old elevator clashes open,
a door too opens, music swells and dies:
The little dancer enters, multiplied,
and the heart lurches, lurches,
she is so delicate against this architecture,
with long pale arms and legs, hair
in a chignon, netted, with a flower,
she so drops through years and histories
as a skylark drops from our zenith overhead
like a stone to the field where her nest is hid:
so she is she, and dance is what she does.

The music starts and the dance instructor
smiles like a cavalier: he calls out steps,
he smiles. She stretches, smiles in return
out of her exhausted, childish face;
she stretches her slim legs one after the other
here and there, extends her pretty arms
into this emptiness, this cold cold air.

And again I am at the bedroom window with Betty.
She has drawn me by the hand to look
through pollarded poplars in the front garden
to the street below filled with marching men
and I hear a tramp of boots in unison
belonging to those men marching, marching,
a march that fills the street, chests thrust out,
arms swinging together and heads held high,
muscular, masculine, men marching
as if on parade, though they are working men,
not soldiers at all, in cloth caps
and working clothes that do not match,
and hobnailed boots, tramp tramp,
they think they are wonderful, yes,
I wonder at them, they're undoubtedly wonderful.
What are they up to? 'They're off to London,'
says Betty. 'They're going to ask for work
those men, they'll ask it the hard way,
They will embarrass the government.'
It is a long way, and where will they sleep?
They are staring ahead as if we understood,
there was no need to lie or represent
what everyone knew. And where do we fit in?
'You're a girl!" says Betty. 'Girls are different.'
What do they do? What else was there?
Betty clucked her tongue and shook her head.
'Your time will come,' my mother said.
The full sad meaning escaped me.

The Shock

The moment he reached into the cold machine
he received a colossal kick or jar or jolt
that burned up his life like paper or oxygen
till a mate threw a switch after four seconds,
though not before he'd cried out 'like a girl',
or thought he'd 'let down' his wife and child, or
wondered who was to blame, if anyone,
until, the current off, he fell on to the floor,
his heart started again, he resumed his life.

Two years on, he'd a scar and a pit in his flesh.
He'd only nightmares now to contend with:
fireworks made him scream, his rage boiled out
when the small child stumbled on the step,
as if he'd die again to hear her cry.

His wife was impatient, even a bit ashamed.
'I don't get it. I mean, all this time!
He dreams he's dying. When's it going to end?'
she said in private to the psychiatrist,
who spoke of bombs and booby traps and guns
making such wounds as his that could persist,
though but one second long, a whole lifetime.
Another year and she would see him changed.
Meanwhile she shouldn't think of right behaviour,
but wait till the mind's wound healed.

The country of suffering she drove home through
was featureless, no one in the fields,
the wolds beyond in cloud.
Look, so she cried. It mattered to no one.
She'd do as she was bid, therefore:
count just for now meaning peripheral,
remember 'a man was more than a Christian':
await, like a cat, the mouse of what and where.

The Pebble

To date, it lies at the door, your pebble with the hole in it,
together with little fingers from the island of Ossabaw,
shoe-button ambers from the Whitby beach,
the San Diego stone with the petrified worm trails,
sea-glass from Narragansett, the big ammonite
I took from a moorland wall. Your pebble alone
aches with recognition.

To date, the rosemary I rooted
at each side of the door has grown by two feet,
Albertine that marvellous rose has climbed to the eaves,
and the clematis Montana wreathed window after window.
It was soon after you returned from the Gulf
I planted the lot, in an effort to anchor my life.
Look how well they have done by that little stone
which aches with recognition!

Admit it all the while to be nothing but a stone
that the seas have tumbled till the middle was run
through: you wore it on your finger like a wedding ring
the day you came home from the war in the Gulf.
Bernini's marble Saint Teresa was something of the same—
pierced by a laughing angel's spear in a long swoon
of bliss and agony. I know the feeling well.
The O mouth in the stone cries out, you start to die a little.

In York Minster

Remember how they said in Aranjuez
in dry Castile that the town trees were prodigies
because there were rivers underground
watering the roots? No rivers run under York:
when they dug a cave under the Minster floor
to pour new footing for the crossing tower
lest it collapse, they found only a drain,
a runnel oozed out of the compressed clay,
runt of the brotherhood Ouse, Seven, Seph,
Riccal, Dove, Foss, Rye, Derwent, Hodge Beck,
that spread upon our plain and keep it green.
If in the crypt you sense that giant trees root here
you err. Above is only stone, bare stone, magnesium
limestone, not wood; and yet the mighty towers
leaf like stone oaks, the window tracery flowers,
the transepts are two boughs, the light on us
is filtered as in a wood, people's voices
arrive with the rustle of birds in the undergrowth,
and I walk in the nave and remember Aranjuez.

At Colonus

Even as we slept, we became aware of
Tearing and munching of grass under our window,
Luscious guzzlings and snorts and gasps.
The came a foldyard cough.

We awoke. Three in the morning
And a handful of stars in the very top
Of the black, black window.
Annihilation, eyelids down, not terminus
Dying, shall I hold you thus?
Pain is that you? Pain? Pain is it,

Who keeps me alive and out of control?
Who was it said I was too calm,
When all the other cheer-up signs were wrong?
Flags, bands, parades, balloons,
Even marriage to the queen?

If I were you, you'd be the death of me.
Such moans and wringing of hands!
I mean to be a hundred and one
And always look after you, Pain.

Annihilation is no excuse.
Even with open lids I just can't see.
What though the scene was much the same,
Still dark and still Colonus,
The old one and the girl
Pretending all was well. At the signal
The old one was carried off,
The girl took up her story,
The famous horses went on eating grass.

Antigone at Colonus

1

A cold religious air blew from the past,
Destined to win. She threw the bedclothes back
And lit the fire each dawn, knowing the worst
That could still happen, scrubbed and cooked
And served his meals, convinced it was no use,
The door stuck so, the windows ran with damp,
The plaster smelled of mould, beetles and silverfish
Scattered like shot when she brought in the lamp.
Not that he cared. Pain kept him alive.
He even liked his eye-holes' ooze and stench.
He kissed the air and cooed 'Antigone!'
Sure she'd hang on. But one day she surprised
A Fury fast asleep behind a hedge,
And packed her things at once, and crept away.

2

Still dark, and still Colonus, still the moor
To thread; the simple necessary path
Soon lost among the scrub and bank of gorse.
Across a hill she waited. Blackness everywhere.
Blackbirds got up and went to work on trills.
A dog barked twice. And then the first light showed
A rough field wall at hand and running wild
As edge between her and the outer world.
But when she climbed that wall and ran to meet
The little that remained, she failed to hear
The rustle of the ambush laid ahead.
Prison was cruel. At intervals she thought
Of walls, their weight, their cool particulars,
The lumpy absolutes that met her need.

3

And days went by before the rescue came.
Since Oedipus was dead for all she knew,
She simply said goodbye and set off home
Along the well-known roads unrecognised
Until she reached the gates, when bugles fussed,
A thousand pigeons burst across the sun
And everybody wept. That wasn't all.
They cleared the streets for dancing, bands struck up,
You couldn't see the rooftops for the flags.
The king's own son ran up and took her hand,
Mad for her love. She raised her eyes and smiled:
Here finally was room for principle,
As she would show him in the days to come,
When she would have her say on martyrdom.

The Sparrowhawk

I look from the glass half of the kitchen door
that frames the garden between its walls
down to the garage that end-blocks the view,
a frame for flowers, plum trees, a little greenhouse,
a bench for summer, stones, gravel, and silence,
lidded with storm clouds blown overhead;
and faintly, faintly, through the double glass,
make out the squawks and thrashing wings
of birds, as twenty sparrows at one go
pour out of the thicket and down to the path
from crumbs on the bird table and bowl to drink from.

Then up and away again in well rehearsed panic,
flushed back to the philadelphus, wild roses, mahonia,
where they gossip in hiding and shiver the leaves,
and swoop out as one again, their wings a-flutter,
grey feathered mêlée on grey paving stones,
landing and pecking and pulling attacks—
when a blackness no bigger than my hand
rockets among them and picks off a sparrow
and zooms up to the sky. The other sparrows shriek
and flee into the thicket and tweet.
And what is this illicit rapture I feel
at silliness dealt with as if by a knife?

Islay Goes To Sleep

I tell her she's lovely. She lifts a foreleg humbly
to show she may be fondled along her brindled chest.
Then she gives way to nibbling and settling her pelt,
her coat, her paws, and tail, and licks her paws
and draws them over and over her muzzle
like a cat, like the cat she once loved.
She arranges her tongue in her mouth
with a slobber and two moans,
and licks beneath a white-haired paw
the black pads, four with a claw each
and the greater pad like the palm of our hand,
and utters a complaint and sighs
and settles her head along her now-folded paws
and looks with her black eyes under her black ears
into nothing, and collapses into the smell of herself
in the soft red fur beneath and the coarse top coat
of grizzled brown, some hairs tipped black;
and arranges her muzzle just one more time,
and closes her eyes and is oblivious

and I think she sleeps as though she were drawn
through water on a canal, a barge among the fields,
or through the air, a glider soaring beyond the hills.

Otherness

I lie on the edge of the incoming light
    as the newspaper drops through the door
        and the newspaper boy
            whistles his way through the gate.
Night still blocks the road.
    The earliest
        cars haven't yet come.
            The colour of soldiers then,
the colour of flags on snow-covered hills
    strikes me unbidden,
        a menace set out on the back of my mind,
            and I think of the ruins I've seen,
the roofless crumbling shells
    above the trafficking sea
        in the path of the Norway wind,
            and I wonder why conscience survives
to make that connection,
    so lively and sad it is still,
        as to why and whom I should mourn.

I lean on the bridge that hoops over the river
    And wonder how fishes survive.
        Do fishes know whether or not
            What they live in is water?
What element lets me still live?
    Do I breathe like a fish in my marriage?
        In husband and children and home?
As a daughter, unmarried, I'd scoff.
    As a wife, now, what have I missed?
        And should I be recognised
            if I stole a boat to sail
down to the ocean purely to explore
    my indifferent element would surge brightly
        sparkling right up to the stubborn horizon.

I sit in a meeting and gaze at the opposite wall
    till the ghost of a onetime door
        shows up on thin plaster and paint,
            and I smile at the thought
that says there's no end,
    and as if there is nowhere constraint.
        And I think of that girl hailing a bus,
            how her sleeve fell back to show
a wrist tattooed with numbers from some diabolical camp—
    normality's double, first-hand,
        at a Bayswater bus-stop in hell, oh long, long ago!
kept handy, in a place for the unexpected that's crammed,
    flooded with explanation at times,
        as the sea rushes in and subsides,
but clean and clear and sweet? No, no, not with our certainties.

Voicing the Air We Breathe

Not a day goes by
but I read you, poetry, poetry,
clutching at words as they pass.
If I grab one, they scatter like mice.
'What have I to say?'
they scream as I touch them.

Not a day goes by
but I hear you, poetry, poetry,
battering the door of the house.
When I open up, there's nobody there.
Mysterious too, mysterious,
the clatter of leaves on the oak—
what is the message? It's Greek.

Not a day goes by
without traces, traces
of something indefinable,
from the wallop of sea on the strand
to a sudden suicidal kiss
from that ploughman I see
ploughing up, ploughing down,
like a knitter knitting an everyday coat
I'll wear in due time—
surprising with otherness, perplexing
flawed knowledge, nevertheless
that which demands an answer,
a special one, not
the long confirmations of the day.

A Word of Acknowledgement

Under rain like this—silky, diaphanous—
common in Skye, where mist swells the straits
and the hills come and go, the Isleornsay
inn where I've stayed comes to mind,
facing the mainland with punctilious gravity,
looking so forthright it won't let go.

As in the 1880s, under rain like this,
the Napier Commission held its enquiry here
into crofters' lives, putting questions,
getting answers and reports in two languages
on high rents, burning thatch, cries in the night, eviction,
and families destitute upon the worthless shore.

Further, believe it, under rain like this,
before the commissioners emerged into the air
and walked back to their ship at the end of the day,
they let a last old man come forward
with his importunate not very relevant say
about his own and his father's appalling century,

when a woman could be snatched off the field,
a fisherman from the shore or asleep in his bed,
all of them gone like smoke, no one knew where.
After years and years, a few came back,
from the Carolinas, mostly. And who they were,
hardly anyone knew, enslaved as they'd been, and aged.

The old man was glad someone at last had listened,
and I'm glad to have read the record of his words.
For crofters' kin, there's been some redress.
I can pay my bill at the inn and speak as I wish
and walk past a hundred hovels, all of them empty, all roofless
under the rain, and write a verse on the matter.

The Sleeve

You took your arm out of its sleeve last night
with a sigh like a train
about to exit
from York's Victorian station,
arc of cast iron, plate glass and air—
leaving so quietly it seems to disappear,
so brilliant that lunette
of expeditionary light
beyond the platforms,

so bright that hand of yours
entering the arc
of the lamp, the tweedy semi-dark
of the sleeve abandoned and falling to the floor
as a building might crumple
in the soundless shockwave
following an explosion.

II

Reasons

There are no reasons worth thinking of,
only the shadows of other worlds that move
like ships out at sea, faintly visible
to watchers on cliffs, who can't identify them,
till boats appear below, keels scrape on shingle,
men ship their oars and hop overboard
into the surf, hauling their boats ashore.
Once on the strand, they stare upward:
they're assessing the risk,
wondering what country this is.

That's the moment when I'll say,
'Let me pass, I know these men.
I speak their language. My father knew them,
as probably did yours.
They may, as you say, have guns,
but I'll go up cautiously.
"Hullo!" I'll say, "Don't shoot!"
I'm old as you see, and a woman.
They'll see for themselves I'm harmless.
"I've been a stranger too," I'll say.
"These people are friends. Friends
is what we have been these eighty years."'

And with any luck they will believe me
They'll smile and settle among us,
and we'll take one another for granted.

Father Felipe

Father Felipe came to talk
to John, who loved Spain.
After an hour I brought in tea,
silver pot on silver tray,
fresh scones, butter, jam,
and put to him a damnfool question:
What was it like (sugar?)
to be a Spaniard (milk?)
in the North Country,
the North Riding of Yorkshire
('so far from home, Father Felipe!'),

and had him answer mournfully
he disliked relativism,
whether Spanish-English,
Catholic-Protestant,
Christian-Muslim, north-south,
man-woman. Father Felipe,
young and scowling,
taught singing to boys.
That was his métier.
He knew where he stood
in music, sung music, choirs.
There was nothing to refute
up there on the moors.

And he looked down, angry.
I said nothing, nodded only,
full of his rebuke,
and thought of the absolutes
he must have lived by
and the harmonies he heard
and taught, and how we lived,
relatively speaking,
complacent, worlds apart.

Studley, 1940

Seventy years ago, my school was here.
Everyone had gone to the war but us—
owners, gardeners, woodsmen, guests.
The peace seemed blasphemous.
We were useless, as the young are.

When winter came, grass froze.
Deer ate the saddles off our bikes,
the little river stood still, its pools
became white moons and stars,
the statues more and more outrageously
gratuitous. One little temple only
came out of its woods when they turned dark,
and the banqueting house—for picnics really—
gave us a view, once we climbed up,
but the great ruins spoke
of winters even more unlucky
and survival as someone's trophy.

No comfort there, though we sought none.
War grumbled in the distance.
Whole cities burned elsewhere. At night
bombs jettisoned from homebound raiders
burst in adjacent fields.
So what were the gardens for? The river
had clearly been straightened,
some weirs put in, for sound.
Frankly, I preferred the rabbit I found,
a baby, deep in grass and hopping with fleas.
Put it back, a teacher said, and I did so,
so it was safe, in that perfection.

Now crowds all year justify the activity.
They walk the walks, view the views,
follow the arrows, read notices,
mouth rectitudes, look happy,
even improved. For myself,
I still have to struggle with the rebuff
I felt then, that being put in my place.

Bread

You take yourself for granted, but if you ask
what I miss most, I'd have to say your bread:
how every loaf roof falls to the knife, its oat
nuggets loading the cut rift; how crust
and rough crumb answer to butter, at breakfast,
with coffee; how teeth crunch on it as I'm fed,
how tongue savours and spit spurts. Your bread
puts me in touch with every common lust.
For trees up here lean blazing on the field,
mountains rise naked from a coloured fur
of leaves like hard embarrassed men, the fall
bursts overhead like rockets. Despite all,
I'm dull with hunger, every sense is sealed,
wanting your bread, the body's integer.

The Pet

I say, 'Go away!' to the dog when she pesters me
and brings the ball to me once too often
when I want to read, and she leaves obediently

but is back in two minutes
having thought of another of our games.
I must have some value, then,
though I can't say what that is,
stranded as I am at the end of life
like a castaway watching ships far out at sea.

Suddenly though she becomes irresistible,
her brilliant black eyes in her brindled pelt
registering a ridiculous amount of regard,
and now it's as though I'm sailing a small boat
among liners and ferries and container ships,
a proper blip upon the radar screen,
and I throw the ball for her one more time.

Bloomsbury Gardens

Looking down on it, you'd be amazed
how empty the garden is—
though doesn't perfection come at a price?—
the price of being unknown
though discovered again and again
through five hundred windows a day—
counting twenty windows to a house
in these Georgian terraces with great names—
Bedford, Russell, Montague—
that make three sides to this garden
of combed gravel, a round lawn
that's perfectly green and shaded
with delicate trees of heaven
hung over flowering bushes.
The space should be crowded with families,
or at least with children, not empty.
I'd be there too, but a friend is waiting
in Russell Square, beyond these end-stop houses,
among the crowds of hurrying students,
tourists, dog-walkers,
pram-pushers, in the public garden
of the square, where there's a café,
broad scuffed walks under plane trees
that are elephantine, eunuch, blotchy,
and benches for old men reading newspapers,
and a big shallow marble basinful of water
filled from freshets a few inches high.
Though it's October, and some trees looked torched
and migrant birds have left
and leaves glide like platters from plane trees,
water still sizzles from the freshets,
each with pigeons dousing their feathers,
squatting and fluttering in the water
until they are soaked. (Aren't they cold?)
I can only stop and admire.
'Why, there you are! Shall we have a coffee?'

Homeless

'I've a coat might fit you. And shoes,'
said my mother. 'What size do you take?'
His toes lay podgy and pink
in the gap between foot sole and upper.
He sat by the kitchen fire
in the stiff snotty coat, small
and bearded like our king,
with a slab of bread and butter
in one hand, a cup of tea in the other.
He was agreeable, I think.
His eye smiled under its lid.

'He'll have a house, never fear,' said Lily.
'Condemned, it is likely, oh yes,
with doors and windows soft with damp
and beetles and silverfish
running for dear life
when his wife brings in the lamp,
and rats twittering in the walls.
For him you could say it's better on the road.'

So many green bells to sleep under
sounding on the edge of the field,
so many bluebells swelling under the trees.
He might lie down by a hedge
that creaked with drought and mice.
He could easily sleep in a barn.
Outside there'll always be stars.

When he left by the back door
I wished I had spoken. Last week
I saw him, much younger and stronger,
holed up in a portal, with a dog this time,
a step from the lights and the traffic,
miles from the ditch and the wood,
also the barn, and the stars,
the same I have never forgotten,
the same I can only describe.

Prey

The cat has brought in a bird,
Quite dead, and the size of a matchbox—
brown and grey feathers, tiny bones,
dangling four-toed feet:
did the cat kill it, or the cold?
If cold, the cat's brought not a trophy

but a phenomenon. She'll mean
'Look what I've found!' and
'There are forces at work on my side!
Acknowledge it! Don't you dare scold!
You'll be scolding God next, or nature!'

I take the corpse outside and wrap it in a leaf.
The cat does not follow. She's given up.
No use mourning, she implies, stalking off.
I hide both leaf and body high
in the dust and debris of the ivy
where she won't retrieve it.
'Five sparrows sold for two farthings,
not one of them forgotten before God,'
I murmur. The cat does not reply.
She hates whim, she hates fantasy.
She can do better than that.

The very next day, no sparrow but a mallard
lies dead on the step, too big to carry.
She has opened his breast and devoured his heart,
and glowers at me from the bushes.

The Colour of Soldiers

The colour of soldiers, the colour of armies in winter
The colour of flags on a hill. Shells
Of houses unroofed two centuries ago
Above the tremendous trafficking sea,
And the people expelled—what true self was lost
That wasn't again to be lost with each new place?
And the songs and legends they took, intact as yet,
And the effort that followed, to be accurate?

The sight of a kiss feels nothing like a kiss.
They say a fish knows nothing of the water.
And yet as happened, someone you barely knew
Turned up in the village trying to elicit
What kind of people we were. I saw our lives
Drawn up—clothes bought, hats and shoes,
And passports, birthdays, calendars, electoral rolls,
House numbers, timetables, surveys—no clue as to
   what we were!

You were always there, engaged on being—
You tell me stoutly, and I have to believe you.
I shan't wait for discovery, here you still are.
Now everyone knows, it's not at all wrong
To wander the world as a stranger. Forget
That girl at the bus-stop with her wrist tattoo
From Auschwitz or Dachau, you hadn't known her.
Though you knew her already, I'm sure.

So a sense of loss, like a door in a wall
Once plastered over, now thinly visible,
Turns into a place for the unexplained,
Floods with knowing as if a war
Needed its histories in order to be clear.
Now and then, as the tide rushes in and subsides
And leaves all clear and clean and sweet,
It follows on, our trophies from violence,
Although to understand it you must live forever.

Waking

A hole in the air off the isle of Lundy,
a hole in a head on the pillow this night,
holes in the air, in the head, one in the other, containing
a cauldron of black and white puffins aflash,
aflash as they whirr and soar and plummet,
each like a well-flung bottle with trailing ribbon of feet
and a red and blue lozenge of a beak
in a white head that's striped through the eye.

The last hour of night. The windows pale.
Quiet. The milkman hasn't yet clanked up the path
nor the postman or newsboy come tramping,
the letterbox lid hasn't yet clacked.
The geese haven't flown over the gardens,
wings creaking like doors, giving each other advice.
True, the sky has winched a crack
of clear while line over the rooftops,
true that pigeons clatter up from the ash trees
(but now they clatter back).
A blackbird practises one phrase and then another.
Has someone spoken? No one.
Was that the telephone? No.

The puffins lift off from rocks by the sea,
from the floor of the bucket of mind
and the hole in the air off Lundy:
till, as they fling down the sky just this once
again and rashly mount to summit grass,
cramp strikes human legs, with sling-shot accuracy.
Some watcher on the cliffs has got me.
I slip from my bed and hobble the cold floor
(puffins falling through the enormous air),
and, yes, my legs come gradually free,
and words fly out once more
like puffins after winter storms spent on the great sea,
clumping together in rafts: in April
they break camp and whirr to the greening land

and nest on cliffs in burrows, and hatch their young;
and I that after all have no part in their kind
watch the milkman come, still a youngish man,
serving these houses like a messenger.

Ataraxia

About six in the morning, light lemonish in the sky,
frost hemming pantiles and roof-trees
corralling leafy lawn, leafless sycamore, crab apple,
benches, the table for breakfast in July.
The big bare sycamore's hung with a dozen pigeons,
feathers puffed in the frost, plus—from an old gale—
two plastic bags. Now the sky's a blue in which
two seagull squadrons wheel in from the North Sea
fifty miles off, one overhead, the other diagonal.

Now new clear light fills garden between its walls.
A man emerges on a balcony, yawns, retires.
The gulls will be floating on the river now
among mallards and greylags, even a swan or two
(always food for a bird on the river).
But six or eight blackbirds sit in the crab-apple,
eating red apples each the size of a cherry.
And now there's a magpie among them,
flash madam, black, white, burly,
screeching. The blackbirds scatter.

The old woman in Number Ten looks on.
She's at the end of her tether.

Amazing Memories of Childhood

1. The Precipice

Somewhere inside our present tense
we're on a mountain, headed north
along a pass, in snow.
We've driven all day, you, I, the boy,
no room to spare
in this three-wheeler, two-stroke car,
with forward, hatchlike door.
(Last night men tossed it up a bank.
We hauled it down intact at breakfast-time.)
Now, in a grand parade of cars,
we creep again through snow—
look out though now,
we leave our crawling traffic line
and spin out to a precipice—
stone walls run past, wheels grip
suddenly on broken ice,
and turn us back. We whirl,
and battle back in line, and laugh,
waking the baby on my lap,
who innocently starts to clap.

By a miracle in our old age now
we lie snow-haired in our one bed
and in imagination skid
through a traffic that comes up
to shunt us over that last cliff.
Unheard, my ancient love, I ask
how long it will be till you laugh.

2. Fog

Riding back from hounds that afternoon,
having lost the hunt and all its followers to fog,
including George, my George, on his bicycle:
ignorant of where I was, or whom to ask,
everyone warm and indoors by the fire,
and sure I was a fool, nine years old, still ignorant,
my pony clattering under me aware
how much a fool I was: when a man loomed
out of the dark, I asked the way of him
and he pointed with his stick, as if it were obvious.
And so we jogged and walked and jogged,
another hour, till we were on the green.
Half a mile more and there was my home
stiff in its brick wall, the stable in the yard,
fodder in the manger, harness off, her blanket on,
then lights, voices, warmth, some milk.
I took my boots off, fell upon my bed and slept.
And when I woke, it was to find
someone had covered me and I was warm.

3. The Row

I am older by far than ever he became
yet the crack and jostle of the planks
under his wheels are with me still and also
the splintering of the railings on one side
and the awful splash that afternoon
when he drove off the wooden bridge
into the swollen estuary tide
and drowned on the way to Seaton Carew—
though he came back in time for the news,
whistling, and carefully put away the car
as if the shouts and slammed doors at lunchtime
had never happened, as if
the wooden bridge on the way to Seaton Carew
would never need to be replaced,
or he'd not go on to other cars on other roads,
and as if he would live for ever.

4. The Storm

Juddering, heaving blasts
through window frames and doors,
puffing chimney smoke
back into the room,
streaming rain on glass,
trying to heave the house
up into the air
past morning and all afternoon
flying like a bird
until the ten-foot garden wall
crumbled and fell flat
beyond the flower beds—
chunks of ancient, ancient
greyish clump-fired bricks
and lengths of coping stone
fallen with a thump
and look, too, miles beyond
house and garden all
the unknown neighbourhood
formed in a single view:
flagstone paths still wet,
sheds cocked by the wind,
fencing pushed askew
garden gates unhinged;
till the four o'clock goods train
came out of the earth far-off,
hooting as usual, puffing loud,
trundle of goods wagons
barely imaginable, now seen,
heard quite as usual;
dusk seen too, dusk as usual, still,
as I crept, havering, over the bricks,
wire netting, fences strewn
over cabbages, dead stalks and flowers
as far as the culvert, empty now,
as the lights flicked on,
showing families gathering for tea,
I gazed at them unseen, unsure
of where we fitted in.

5. Lowna

The car stopped on the greenwood edge,
recognition cracks open a door:
the rustle of the beck breaking over rocks—
the sight of it then, dark little Dove
running between banks clothed with ribbon
leaves and small bobbing daffodils,
thousand on thousand of them—

till just where birch departs
from stands of ash, oak, sycamore,
and used to meet the path
from the Quaker burial-ground,
high-walled and padlocked then
behind a wooden gate,
a kingfisher in the alders below
watches the water, and with a flash
of bright blue-green
wings it upstream, as eighty years earlier.

The daffodils are thicker now than when
we children took our armfuls back to school
and posted shoe-boxes of them home
wrapped in damp newspaper.
Of course they got there dead,
and word came back, dull as a lump of mud:
'What were you thinking of?
Next time let them be, lest they die out.'

Warned off by notices, no one now picks the flowers.
The burial-ground also is unlocked: a notice there
explains why Quakers were buried
outside the parish. There are benches inside
for comfort while you contemplate;
that makes me glad, but I am glad also
we plundered these woods once:
the pleasures of piracy sweetly return.
Plundering, not thinking twice,
no pieties bothered us:
our greed looks only natural now.

6. The Hare

Leaving the house behind, and the trees,
we'd walked down to the bottom land
of salt meadows, marshes, dunes,
where beck looped out towards the sea
and sea-smell met ammonia
from the vast chemical works on the estuary.
A Saturday shoot. A line of men, guns cocked, stationary.
Wives, children (I was one), in a line of beaters,
moving over rough ground at an angle to them.
October, a sickle moon in the blue, barely visible.

A crackle of guns. The beaters re-form,
again over rough ground. Again, gunfire.
And then, a scream like an arrow through the head.
Two minutes. Another scream, and a single shot.
We broke. Somebody cried. A man walked back.
'A hare,' he said. 'She'll scream like that.'

In a couple of years, the barrage balloons,
ack-ack units and the boom of guns,
seachlights, bombs, ruins, policeman with a sack
of human parts, nights in the cellar, all four of us.

The pity of it, the pity! What had we been thinking of?

7. After Her Funeral

After the funeral, my father looked back
over their sixty years
in search of a reason for remorse.
Humming and whistling, at last he hit
on their tour of the Highlands together,
with Billy Miles, in their first car,
two-seater Swift with rear dickey
that opened like a lid.

My father was driving, her turn in the dickey,
Billy inside, snug, smug and chatty,
when a storm broke over Glencoe.
She was drenched forthwith,
while Billy chatted on under cover, dry,
warm and quite oblivious.
'How could I do that to her?'
my father asked me: 'Why let that Billy
blab on and stay dry, dry and under cover,
While she was soaked to the skin?'

I'd never heard that story before, I said.
There was nothing to forgive.
She'd always said he was lovable,
beloved, an excellent man.
And I shivered, feeling the desolation
forming around me, its chill and its wet,
and thought of their one-time rows,
hurled glasses and jugs, shouts in the night,
grapes chucked on the fire like money:
warfare that made them distinct
and their lives in harmony.

8. In Antwerp Once

Once, returning home from Brittany,
in Antwerp, making for the ferry
for Harwich and the North Country,
on a wide ancient cobbled street,
with tramlines, buses, other cars,
my father suddenly speeded up.
Faster yet and faster (what on earth for?),
big foot down on floor,
back braced, hands tight on wheel,
right across traffic, swerving,
hurtling, minute after minute,
breath taken in, out, again,
sharp as a pain, until
from the back seats where I sat with him
my brother reached forward,
reached the ignition key, turned it,
turned the engine off.

Engine cut, brake found,
we shuddered to a halt.
Breathing, in, breathing out,
engine restarted, nothing said,
never spoken of,
back on the right hand side of the street,
we motored to the ferry.

9. Those Evenings

Those evenings by the bedroom fire
my father coughed and read.
Outside the snow fell into my eyes
flat flake on flake on flake
running clear upon the glass,
running and vanishing.
A crimson pit inside my head
formed and reformed as hell
night by night by night.
Nightly by the bedroom fire
my father coughed and read.

10. At Duncombe

June, ten at night, still light in the sky,
periphery dark with woods,
sixty little girls asleep, but not I.
At last, at last the forbidden stair
up to the huge forbidden roof:
I looked down from the parapet
on to the tops of elms below—
sea of green from a top deck
ship's chimney-stacks like these,
those steel of course, these, brick and clay,
and over us all the pale pale sky
quaking, shivering, flashing with coloured light—
pink, green—perhaps it always did, this late—
dark after all along the earth's rim
where owls hooted, one to the other
in woods across the river,
with cows munching somewhere in the dark
and the honey smell of elm.

Then voices. The scene ignites. Girls,
our headmistress. So I hid. The skies flickered.
I glided to the stair, went down,
quickly, unseen, to my room,
finding my bed in the dark, the empty one of five.

At breakfast, talk dwelt on
something called 'Northern Lights'.
I nodded, said nothing, felt outwitted.

11. Fairbanks, Alaska

When someone was having his say
on Fairbanks, Alaska,
and the fearsome quality of Alaskan cold,
my mother, I recall, countered
with her own version of extremes,
the height of the waves on Bondi Beach,
how she nearly drowned in them once,
and how peaceful it was, that act of dying,
before she was rescued and revived.

Listening, I forgot everything that had been said
about Fairbanks, Alaska,
in favour of her presence, the way she smiled,
having brilliantly taken the floor.

12. Hindenburg

How many times have I crossed the Atlantic?—
east to west and west to east,
by ship first, then by air—it feels like a hundred-hundred times
and I've survived—it shouldn't amaze me;
no, it's more the done thing—people I meet now
have all been there, all know New York
for example—East River, Hudson, Palisades …

More than such commonplace experiences
I sharply recall an airship drifting slowly, silently
over our garden in County Durham,
R-one-hundred-and-one, monstrous, rigid, silvery, dirigible
that chugged on its way
when propellers at last engaged.

At its end one such airship, huge, dirigible, the Hindenburg,
burst into flames and withered
over Lakehurst, New Jersey (before the war, this was),
bodies falling through the air as at Nine Eleven,
as unbelievably—before the war, though,
after which, as I always say, anything could happen.

Also by Two Rivers poets:

David Attwooll, *The Sound Ladder* (2015)
Paul Bavister, *Miletree* (1996)
Paul Bavister, *Glass* (1998)
Paul Bavister, *The Prawn Season* (2002)
Kate Behrens, *The Beholder* (2012)
Kate Behrens, *Man with Bombe Alaska* (2016)
Adrian Blamires, *The Effect of Coastal Processes* (2005)
Adrian Blamires, *The Pang Valley* (2010)
Adrian Blamires & Peter Robinson (eds.), *The Arts of Peace* (2014)
Joseph Butler, *Hearthstone* (2006)
David Cooke, *A Murmuration* (2015)
Terry Cree, *Fruit* (2014)
Jane Draycott and Lesley Saunders, *Christina the Astonishing* (1998)
Jane Draycott, *Tideway* (2002)
Claire Dyer, *Eleven Rooms* (2013)
John Froy, *Eggshell: A Decorator's Notes* (2007)
David Greenslade, *Zeus Amoeba* (2009)
A. F. Harrold, *Logic and the Heart* (2004)
A. F. Harrold, *Flood* (2009)
A. F. Harrold, *The Point of Inconvenience* (2013)
Ian House, *Cutting the Quick* (2005)
Ian House, *Nothing's Lost* (2014)
Gill Learner, *The Agister's Experiment* (2011)
Kate Noakes, *The Wall Menders* (2009)
Tom Phillips, *Recreation Ground* (2012)
Victoria Pugh, *Mrs Marvellous* (2008)
Peter Robinson, *English Nettles and Other Poems* (2010)
Peter Robinson (ed.), *Reading Poetry: An Anthology* (2011)
Peter Robinson (ed.), *A Mutual Friend: Poems for Charles Dickens* (2012)
Peter Robinson, *Foreigners, Drunks and Babies: Eleven Stories* (2013)
Lesley Saunders, *Her Leafy Eye* (2009)
Lesley Saunders, *Cloud Camera* (2012)
Susan Utting, *Houses Without Walls* (2006)
Susan Utting, *Fair's Fair* (2012)
Jean Watkins, *Scrimshaw* (2013)

Two Rivers Press has been publishing in and about Reading since 1994. Founded by the artist Peter Hay (1951–2003), the press continues to delight readers, local and further afield, with its varied list of individually designed, thought-provoking books.